New Poems by Richard Le Gallienne

Richard Thomas Gallienne was born in Liverpool on 20th January, 1866.

His first job was in an accountant's office, but this was quickly abandoned to pursue his first love as a professional writer. His first work, My Ladies' Sonnets, was published in 1887.

In 1889 he became, for a brief time, literary secretary to Wilson Barrett the manager, actor, and playwright. Barrett enjoyed immense success with the staging of melodramas, which would later reach a peak with the historical tragedy The Sign of the Cross (1895).

Le Gallienne joined the staff of The Star newspaper in 1891, and also wrote for various other papers under the pseudonym 'Logroller'. He contributed to the short-lived but influential quarterly periodical The Yellow Book, published between 1894 and 1897.

His first wife, Mildred Lee, died in 1894 leaving their daughter, Hesper, in his care.

In 1897 he married the Danish journalist Julie Norregard. However, the marriage would not be a success. She left him in 1903 and took their daughter Eva to live in Paris. They were eventually divorced in June 1911.

Le Gallienne now moved to the United States and became resident there.

On 27th October 1911, he married Mrs. Irma Perry, whose marriage to her first cousin, the painter and sculptor Roland Hinton Perry, had been dissolved in 1904. Le Gallienne and Irma had known each other for many years and had written an article together a few years earlier in 1906.

Le Gallienne and Irma lived in Paris from the late 1920s, where Irma's daughter Gwen was by then an established figure in the expatriate bohème. Le Gallienne also added a regular newspaper column to the frequent publication of his poems, essays and other articles.

By 1930 Le Gallienne's book publishing career had virtually ceased. During the latter years of that decade Le Gallienne lived in Menton on the French Riviera and, during the war years, in nearby Monaco. His house was commandeered by German troops and his handsome library was nearly sent back to Germany as bounty. Le Gallienne managed a successful appeal to a German officer in Monaco which allowed him to return to Menton to collect his books.

To his credit Le Gallienne refused to write propaganda for the local German and Italian authorities, and financially was often in dire need. On one occasion he collapsed in the street due to hunger.

Richard Thomas Gallienne died on 15th September 1947. He is buried in Menton in a grave whose lease is, at present, due to expire in 2023.

Index of contents

I

THE CRY OF THE LITTLE PEOPLES

The Cry of the Little Peoples went up to God in vain;
The Czech, and the Pole, and the Finn, and the Schleswig Dane.

We ask but a little portion of the green, ambitious earth;
Only to sow and sing and reap in the land of our birth.

We ask not coaling stations, nor ports in the China seas.
We leave to the big child-nations such rivalries as these.

We have learned the lesson of time, and we know three things of worth;
Only to sow and sing and reap in the land of our birth.

O leave us our little margins, waste ends or land and sea,
A little grass, and a hill or two, and a shadowing tree;

O leave us our little rivers that sweetly catch the sky,
To drive our mills, and to carry our wood, and to ripple by.

Once long ago, as you, with hollow pursuit of fame.
We filled all the shaking world with the sound of our name

But now are we glad to rest, our battles and boasting done,
Glad just to sow and sing and reap in our share of the sun.

Of this O will ye rob us,—with a foolish mighty hand,
Add, with such cruel sorrow, so small a land to your land?

So might a boy rejoice him to conquer a hive of bees,
Overcome ants in battle,—we are scarcely more mighty than these—

So might a cruel heart hear a nightingale singing alone,
And say, "I am mighty! See how the singing stops with a stone!"

Yea, he were mighty indeed, mighty to crush and to gain;
But the bee and the ant and the bird were the mighty of brain.

And what shall you gain if you take us and bind us and beat us with thongs,
And drive us to sing underground in a whisper our sad little songs?

Forbid us the very use of our heart's own nursery tongue—
Is this to be strong, ye nations, is this to be strong?

Your vulgar battles to fight, and your grocery conquests to keep,
For this shall we break our hearts, for this shall our old men weep?

What gain in the day of battle—to the Russ, to the German, what gain,
The Czech, and the Pole, and the Finn, and the Schleswig Dane?

The Cry of the Little Peoples goes up to God in vain.
For the world is given over to the cruel sons of Cain;

The hand that would bless us is weak, and the hand that would break us is strong,
And the power of pity is nought but the power of a song.

The dreams that our fathers dreamed to-day are laughter and dust,
And nothing at all in the world is left for a man to trust.

Let US hope no more, or dream, or prophesy, or pray,
For the iron world no less will crash on its iron way;

And nothing is left but to watch, with a helpless, pitying eye.
The kind old aims for the world, and the kind old fashions die.

CHRISTMAS IN WAR-TIME

I

This is the year that has no Christmas Day,
Even the little children must be told
That something sad is happening far away—
Or, if you needs must play,
As children must,
Play softly, children, underneath your breath!
For over our hearts hangs low the shadow of death,
Those hearts to you mysteriously old,
Grim grown-up hearts that ponder night and day
On the straight lists of broken-hearted dead.
Black narrow lists no tears can wash away,
Reading in which one cries out here and here
And falls into a dream upon a name.
Be happy softly, children, for a woe
Is on us, a great woe for little fame,—
Ah! in the old woods leave the mistletoe,
And leave the holly for another year,
Its berries are too red.

II

And lovers, like to children, will not you
Cease for a little from your kissing mirth.
Thinking of other lovers that must go
Kissed back with fire into the bosom of earth,—
Ah! in the old woods leave the mistletoe,
Be happy softly, lovers, for you too
Shall be as sad as they another year.
And then for you the holly be berries of blood,
And mistletoe strange berries of bitter tears.
Ah! lovers, leave you your beatitude,
Give your sad eyes and ears
To the far griefs of neighbour and of friend,
To the great loves that find a little end.
Long loves that in a sudden puff of fire
With a wild thought expire.

III

And you, ye merchants, you that eat and cheat.
Gold-seeking hucksters in a noble land,
Think when you lift the wine up in your hand
Of a fierce vintage tragically red,
Red wine of the hearts of English soldiers dead,
Who ran to a wild death with laughing feet—

That we may sleep and drink and eat and cheat.

Ah! you brave few that fight for all the rest,
And die with smiling faces strangely blest,
Because you die for England—O to do
Something again for you,
In this great deed to have some little part;
To send so great a message from the heart
Of England that one man shall be as ten.
Hearing how England loves her Englishmen!
Ah! think you that a single gun is fired
We do not hear in England. Ah! we hear.
And mothers go with proud unhappy eyes
That say: It is for England that he dies,
England that does the cruel work of God,
And gives her well-beloved to save the world.
For this is death like to a woman desired,
For this the wine-press trod.

IV

And, England, when forgot this passing woe,
Because of all your captains, strength on strength.
Think too, when the sure end has come at length,
Victory for England—for God means it so—
Be strong in kindness for the little dead,
The stubborn tribe that could not understand,
But, child-like, fought the purposes of Time;
England, so strong to slay, be strong to spare
England, have courage even to forgive,
Give back the little nation leave to live.
To shear its sheep and grow its lazy corn,—
Children there are that must be whipped to grow,
And some small children must be whipped with fire.

V

And you in churches, praying this Christmas morn,
Pray as you never prayed that this may be
The little war that brought the great world peace;
Undazzled with its glorious infamy,
O pray with all your hearts that war may cease.
And who knows but that God may hear the prayer.
So it may come about next Christmas Day
That we shall hear the happy children play
Gladly aloud, unmindful of the dead,
And watch the lovers go
To the old woods to find the mistletoe.
But this year, children, if you needs must play,

Play very softly, underneath your breath;
Be happy softly, lovers, for great Death
Makes England holy with sorrow this Christmas Day;
Yes! in the old woods leave the mistletoe,
And leave the holly for another year—
Its berries are too red.

Christmas, 1899

THE ILLUSION OF WAR

War
I abhor,
And yet how sweet
The sound along the marching street
Of drum and fife, and I forget
Wet eyes of widows, and forget
Broken old mothers, and the whole
Dark butchery without a soul.

Without a soul—save this bright drink
Of heady music, sweet as hell;
And even my peace-abiding feet
Go marching with the marching street,
For yonder yonder goes the fife,
And what care I for human life!
The tears fill my astonished eyes
And my full heart is like to break,
And yet 'tis all embannered lies,
A dream those little drummers make.

O it is wickedness to clothe
Yon hideous grinning thing that stalks
Hidden in music, like a queen
That in a garden of glory walks.
Till good men love the thing they loathe.
Art, thou hast many infamies.
But not an infamy like this.
O snap the fife and still the drum,
And show the monster as she is.

Soldier going to the war—
Will you take my heart with you,
So that I may share a little
In the famous things you do?

Soldier going to the war—
If in battle you must fall,
Will you, among all the faces,

See my face the last of all?

Soldier coming from the war—
Who shall bind your sunburnt brow
With the laurel of the hero,
Soldier, soldier—vow for vow!

Soldier coming from the war—
When the street is one wide sea,
Flags and streaming eyes and glory—
Soldier, will you look for me?

II

THE HIDDEN LAND

He sat by the side of the lonely hill,
A figure strangely sad and still,
And whatever bird or bee went by,
Or flaunting, floating butterfly,
He took no heed, but sat on still,
Silent and sad by that lonely hill.
Only sometimes his tattered hand
Would stroke a flute that for years had been
His sad companion in many a land—
Thinking of all they two had seen.
A faded, smiling, withered thing.
He sat alone by the lonely hill
There was nothing quite in the world so still.

It was that happy time of day
When children troop from school to play,
And as the minstrel sat so still,
Children came laughing up the hill.
His face was beautiful and good,
The little children understood
Why he sat there so sad and still.
With his lonely flute by the lonely hill,
And understood him too the birds;
The wild birds from the echoing wood
Nestled about his hands and knees.
Blue butterflies were in his hair.
And, crowding at his lips, the bees
Stole all the honey of his words.

The children, as they ran up hill,
Stood round the man that sat so still.
And peered into his eyes,

And saw the bees and the butterflies,
And wondered at the birds.
They saw too in his withered hand
The ancient flute that had been his friend
In many an ancient land.
He had sat silent, nor had cared
For bee or butterfly or bird;
But, when the children came,
And crowded round his knees,
He opened his blue eyes,
Young as the morning skies,
And smiled the love of God
Into those young young eyes.

Then all the children danced and sang,
And, like the butterflies,
Kissed his old hair, and begged him play
On that old flute of his—
To pay him with a kiss.

"Children," said he, "what shall I sing
To such young hearts as yours,
What shall I sing to such small ears
That have not heard the years?
Tell me, what shall I sing to you—
Shall I sing the song of the bird
As it pipes first up to its mother's face?
Shall I sing you the song unheard
Of the opening rose in the morning light,
Or the little whispered word
The baby says to its mother's breast
In the hush of the fragrant night?
What shall I sing to such small ears
That have not heard the years?"

The children said: "O sing us the song
Of the rainbow in the sky!
Sing us the song of the bees and the birds,
And the song of the dragon-fly,—
The Song of the Beautiful Words."

He set the flute to his lips and blew
A little laughing note or two;
"Children," he said, "I will play for you
The song of the Hidden Land,
It lies just yonder under the moon,
Where the soft-winged moths are born,
It is made of dew and daisies and dreams,
And it vanishes at morn.

Dear children, will you come with me
To that Hidden Land, and you shall see
How they make the blue of the sky,
How they make the dragon-fly,
You shall see the rainbow born.
Children, will you come with me?
Children, will you come with me?"

And he blew strange notes through that flute of his,—
A butterfly, a star, a kiss—
Strange sounds like growing grass or birds,
Ah! far more beautiful than words:
In that battered flute was the sound of the sea.
The song of the wind in the April tree.
The song of the humming humming bee
The song of each beautiful thing that flies,
Looks just once in your face—and dies.

"Children," he said, "will you come with me?"
"Children," he said, "will you come with me?"
And the children danced, and each little hand
Took his,—and they went to that Hidden Land.

BALLAD OF THE DEAD LOVER

Deep in the middle of the wood,
Her love lies in his narrow house,
With daisies for his winding sheet,
Beneath the swaying boughs.

Birds peck and pipe, and sunlit leaves
Dreamily flicker o'er his sleep;
But Margaret in her lonely tower,
What can she do but weep?

The dead man sleeps, his aching heart
Aches now no more; the world has passed
Out from his eyes and ears; he sleeps,
He is at peace at last,

Autumn and winter—falling leaves,
And softly falling falling snow—
The dead man slept, nor moved nor dreamed,
Nor anything did know.

But, with the coming of the spring—
Was it the singing of some bird?
Or the sap moving, or the flowers?—
The dead man sighed and stirred.

Deep in the aromatic mould,
A sound had pierced to his deaf ears;
It was not bird, nor rustling leaf—
The sound of falling tears,

Margaret, in her lonely bower.
Lay on her pillow weeping sore,
When, in the hollow night, there fell
Three knocks upon her door.

"Who knocks! who knocks!" she cried in fear;
His voice made answer, "It is I!"
"O God, it was an evil dream,
My love, you did not die!!"

Open she flung the bolted door—
"O love, at last you are come back!"
He stood, with matted daisied hair,
His coffin on his back.

"O can you say the Holy Name?
Or are you some unhallowed sprite
Who takes my dead love's sacred form
To damn me with to-night?"

The dead man spake the Holy Name;
"Your own true love am I," he said,
"I came because I heard your tears
Falling on my green bed."

She took his head upon her knee,
And called him love and very fair,
And with a golden comb she combed
The grave-dust from his hair.

And many a deep heart-broken word,
Waiting and aching to be said.
Spake these sad lovers each to each.
The living and the dead.

Too soon along the eastern sky
The scarlet flower of morning glows,
And faint across the sleeping world
Horizon to horizon crows.

The dead man heard the sound that warns
The errant spirit of the day;
"Adieu, my Margaret, adieu!
I may no longer stay.

"But, ere I go, this promise give—
For me you must no longer weep,
Only be glad that I at last
Have fallen safe asleep.

"Yea, bring your laughter to my grave,
There in the middle of the wood,—
It fills with roses when you laugh.
And, when you weep, with blood."

And then the dead man went his way
Beneath the swaying forest boughs,
And laid him in his winding sheet
Within his narrow house.

THE WIFE FROM FAIRYLAND

Her talk was all of woodland things,
Of little lives that pass
Away in one green afternoon,
Deep in the haunted grass;

For she had come from fairyland,
The morning of a day
When the world that still was April
Was turning into May.

Green leaves and silence and two eyes-
'Twas so she seemed to me,
A silver shadow of the woods.
Whisper and mystery.

I looked into her woodland eyes,
And all my heart was hers,
And then I led her by the hand
Home up my marble stairs;

And all my granite and my gold
Was hers for her green eyes,
And all my sinful heart was hers
From sunset to sunrise;

I gave her all delight and ease
That God had given to me,
I listened to fulfil her dreams.
Rapt with expectancy.

But all I gave, and all I did,
Brought but a weary smile

Of gratitude upon her face;
As though a little while,

She loitered in magnificence
Of marble and of gold,
And waited to be home again
When the dull tale was told.

Sometimes, in the chill galleries,
Unseen, she deemed, unheard,
I found her dancing like a leaf
And singing like a bird.

So lone a thing I never saw
In lonely earth or sky,
So merry and so sad a thing.
One sad, one laughing, eye.

There came a day when on her heart
A wildwood blossom lay.
And the world that still was April
Was turning into May.

In the green eyes I saw a smile
That turned my heart to stone:
My wife that came from fairyland
No longer was alone.

For there had come a little hand
To show the green way home,
Home through the leaves, home through the dew,
Home through the greenwood—home.

BALLAD OF THE SINFUL LOVER

Four years he sinned, because she died—
With base corroding anodyne
He numbed the noble pain in him,
Four years he herded with the swine.

And then at last he died, and went,
With hurry of immortal feet,
To seek in the Eternal Life
The face that he had died to meet.

Up all the stairways of the sky
Laughing he ran, at every door
Of the long corridors of heaven
He knocked, and cried out "Heliodore!"

In shining rooms sat the sweet saints,
Each at her little task of joy;
Old eyes, all young again with heaven.
Watched angel girl and angel boy.

And o'er the fields of Paradise,
Scattered like flowers, the lovers passed,
All rainbows—saying each to each
Heaven's two words: "At last! At last!"

But nowhere in that place of peace
Found he the face that was his own,
Till, on a sudden, by a stream
He found her sitting all alone.

With outstretched hands, he cried her name;
She turned on him her quiet eyes:
"Who art thou that so foul with sin
Darest to walk in Paradise?"

Amazed, he answered: "If I sinned,
My sin was sorrow for thy sake;
The pain, O Hehodore, the pain!
I sinned—O lest my heart should break."

"I know thee not," the saint replied,
"Thy sorrow is all changed to sin;"
And, moving towards a golden door,
She turned away, and entered in.

THE SILVER GIRL

Whiter than whiteness was her breast,
And softer than new fallen snow,
So pure a peace, so deep a rest,
Yet purer peace below.

Her face was like a moon-white flower
That sways upon an ivory stem,
Her hair a whispering silver shower.
Each foot a silver gem.

And in a fair white house of dreams.
With hallowed windows all of pearl,
She sat amid the haunted gleams,
That little silver girl;

Sat singing songs of snowy white,

And watched all day, with soft blue eyes.
Her white doves flying in her sight,
And fed her butterflies.

Then when the long white day was passed,
The white world sleeping in the moon.
White bed, and long white sleep at last—
She will not waken soon.

MARGARET

This is the little Margaret
That dropped from the stars,
Her face is fair as those that look
Through golden bars
Down on the earth
At sunsetting.

Her brow is like some holy pearl
From the deep Indian sea,
Her eyes are only just less blue
Than they are true,
Violets all blue and dew.

Her hair is like some costly thing
From fairyland,
I dare not touch her golden hair
With the most reverent hand,
I dare not look into her eyes
With these of mine,
Lest I should sully those pure deeps,
Calm and divine.

Yet, little Margaret, were I to look
Long, long enough, who knows
But the pure light that flows
Up from your maiden soul
Through those pure wells,
Might with its gentle urgence
Wash my soul;

As men grow pure in reading some pure book,
And only sweetness may surround the rose.

O little Margaret
That dropped from the stars,
Some day the prince will come from fairyland
And take your hand,
And lead you back once more

To all that fairyland from which you came.
To the strange seas so holy and so calm,
Where deep in the ocean of his love,
Your face, his pearl.
Shall feel his shadow o'er you.
Like some palm
That grows by the deep deep Indian sea,
And loves some pearl
Rocking and shimmering thousand leagues below;
And you shall go
Back to the flower-beds
Where grew your eyes,
And to those morning skies
From which you fell,
Our little Margaret
That dropped from the stars.

RED ROSE OF MARGARET

Red rose of Margaret,
Here in my book you lie,
Red as her lips and fragrant yet.
Dead rose that can never die;
Margaret gathered one red rose, and another red rose!

"As long as any rose is red
On this little rose-hung tree.
As long as willow leaves are green.
Shall I be true to thee."
So vowed I unto Margaret and Margaret unto me.

"As long as this little stream shall run
Through the quiet willows here,
Out of the shadow into the sun,
Shall Margaret be dear;
Yea, though the stream should dry and the willows die, and the grass grow sere.

"Yet shall I not forget.
Though the sun should fail,
The holy face of Margaret,
Pale as a pearl is pale;
And change shall change all else, but over this
it shall not prevail.

"And as true as I to Margaret
To me shall Margaret be,
And some day we shall stand again
By that little rose-hung tree,
And each, with a rose in the hand, shall say:

'I was faithful unto thee,'"

LA FOLIE

Half fun and half sorrow
Is La Folie,
There is no to-morrow
With La Folie;
And 'tis laugh while you may,
And weep when you must,
For we've only to-day,
And to-morrow we're dust-
Says La Folie.

Half good and half evil
Is La Folie,
Beware of the devil
In La Folie;
'Tis be good when you must,
And laugh all you can,
And put not your trust
In your enemy, man—
Says La Folie.

Half tears and half laughter
Is La Folie,
O what comes after
For La Folie!
And 'tis give him your heart
Like a woman true,
And watch him break it
In half for you—
Says La Folie.

WEEP, MOTHER OF LOVE!

(AFTER CATULLUS)

Weep, Mother of Love! Weep, Baby-Boy of Arrows!
And weep all men that have a tear to shed!
Because—alas!—the sparrow of all sparrows,
The sparrow of my little girl, is dead.

O it was sweet to hear him twitter-twitter
In the dear bosom where he made his nest!
Lesbia, sweetheart, who shall say how bitter
This grief to us—so small to all the rest?

For Lesbia loved no less that little bird,
Nor less was loved, than mother loves her daughter,
Or daughter mother; would you could have heard
His tiny voice, pretty as falling water!

And in no other bosom would he sing,
But sometimes sitting here and sometimes there,
On one bough and another, would he sing,—
Faithful to Lesbia—as I am to her.

He, little bird, must go, as go the flowers,
Down the dark road by which no man returns;
O curses on the black strength that devours
The beauty of life, and all its music burns

Foul shades of Orcus, evil you befall
'Tis true you smote her little sparrow dead—
But this you did to Lesbia worse than all:
You made her eyes with weeping—O so red!

THE DAYS OF DISTANCE AND THE NIGHTS APART

(AFTER HAFIZ—ODE 192)

The days of distance and the nights apart
Are at an end,
All the long lonely winter of the heart
Is at an end:
No more for ever shall the autumn gloom,
No more for ever shall December freeze,
For lo! the sweet swift-footed April breeze
Fills all the world with fragrance and with bloom—
O my own love and friend,
Our grief is at an end!

Our grief is ended and our joys begun,
We have climbed the night—at last we reach the sun;
And the wide world from pole to pole bright
With the effulgent face of our delight,
From shining end to end.

Deep in the scented shadow of your hair,
I bow my head and weep for very bliss.
So happy I can scarce believe me there,

Too happy even to kiss;
For, love, O most desired and lovely friend.
Through your great locks I see the rising sun.

The solitary night is at an end,
Our morning is begun.

What care I if, for love of your fair face,
To the wide winds my work and place I throw!
My work is just to love you, and the place
Just where you are the only place I know.

Ah! to the wine-shop swiftly let us come,
With happy harp and loud exultant drum.
And with a mighty voice the Saki call—
"Deep cups and many, many cups for all!"
What matter how much money we shall spend.
For, O most lovely and beloved friend.
To-day the grief of HAFIZ, the long grief,
In a wild blessedness beyond belief
Is at an end.

MONODY

This is my lady—pray you wait awhile
Before you lock such beauty underground,
Shut in this dungeon that immortal smile,
And plunder music of its sweetest sound.

This is my lady! Ah! I never told
All that I dare speak now that she is dead;
This is my lady! She who lies so cold,
White as the flowers that wither on her head.

This is my lady! She will never know
How my heart breaks because my heart is hers;
I am the nightingale,—she was the rose!
O give me leave to sing to her, fair sirs!

Ah! rose untimely smitten of the cold,
I bring my burning lute afire with spring,—
So young 'twould turn to blossom faces old!
For thee to listen—scarce is need to sing!

Love, sleeping on with such a silent air—
Awake, for all the land is flower and bird;
What dost thou, little sluggard, sleeping there,
Sleeping as sound as though thou hadst not heard!

O raise thy head!—or, if too weary thou,
Open thine eyes, and nod a little smile,
And in my arms, ah! love, I'll take thee now
And carry thee to God each shining mile.

REQUIEM

Vain, all in vain! O Love, thou dost not hear;
Thou art too lost in sleep to wake again;
In vain my song, in vain the falling tear,
Vain, all in vain!

She will not wake again till Gabriel sings;
For any mortal music we can make.
My lute and I, with these heart-broken strings,
She will not wake.

Sleep then, ah I sleep—if slumber be thy will;
We would not vex thee, though we needs must weep.
Of slumber everlasting take thy fill—
Sleep then, ah! sleep.

THE NORTHERN SPHINX

Sphinx of the North, with subtler smile
Than hers who in the yellow South,
With make-believe mysterious mouth.
Deepens the ennui of the Nile;

And, with no secret left to tell,
A worn and withered old coquette,
Dreams sadly that she draws us yet,
With antiquated charm and spell:

Tell me your secret. Sphinx,—for mine!
What means the colour of your eyes,
Half innocent and all so wise.
Blue as the smoke whose wavering line

Curls upward from the sacred pyre
Of sacrifice or holy death,
Pale twisting wreaths of opal breath,
From fire mounting into fire.

What is the meaning of your hair—
That little fairy palace wrought
With many a grave fantastic thought;
I send a kiss to wander there,

To climb from golden stair to stair,
Wind in and out your cunning bowers,

O garden gold with golden flowers,
O little palace built of hair!

The meaning of your mouth who knows?
O mouth where many meanings meet—
Death kissed it stern, Love kissed it sweet,
And each hath shaped its mystic rose.

Mouth of all sweets, whose sweetness sips
Its tribute honey from all hives.
The sweetest of the sweetest lives,
Soft flowers and little children's lips;

Yet rather learnt its heavenly smile
From Sorrow—God's divinest art—
Sorrow that breaks and breaks the heart,
Yet makes a music all the while.

Ah, what is that within your eyes.
Upon your lips, within your hair,
The sacred art that makes you fair,
The wisdom that hath made you wise.

TO ONE WHO IS BLIND

I said I had forgotten her,
That I had put away
Our memories of Paradise
Until the Judgment Day;

That never more the laughing earth
Should see us hand in hand,
That I long since had shut the door
Of the old fairyland.

Then on a sudden came strange news
Upon the gossip wind
My love of those sweet years ago
Great God—my love was blind!

I said—the news must be a lie,
Cruel as are the years,
They could not be so merciless
To such great eyes as hers.

O little child of long ago,
God grant the news untrue!
Except for one strong selfish thought-
That I may come to you

And sit beside you in the dark,
And, as in Paradise
I gave you all my breaking heart,
Now bring to you—my eyes.

THE HARP-PLAYER

(FOR A PICTURE BY AGNES SLOTT-MOLLER)

What play you on your harp there by the fiord?

Grief that has turned to joy with thinking on,
Heartbreak that comes back singing in a bird,
The kindness now of some old bitter word,
Unhappy things grown happy being gone,
Yea, all the bitter-sweetness of my lord—
It was for this he gave me a harp of gold.

Love took my love—yet gave not his again.

Gave he then nought for all those bitter tears,
Heart loyal, and strong pulses and warm breath,
That loved him verily even unto death,
And all your woman-words in his boy's ears
Was all this given, and given all in vain?

Love gave me for my tears a harp of gold.

TO LYKKE

Lykke, whose name is like some river in Wales
That through the hills says over all day long
Softly its own name, softly, like a song,
Writes it in brimming ripples through long dales,
And whispers it through all its moonlit vales;
I, unfamiliar with your Danish tongue,
Say your name over, over, all day long—
Lykke and Lykke—like the nightingales.

Born of two arts in union, well they knew
That made you, Lykke, all of burning love,
To coil the softest sunshine for your hair,
And where the bluest flowers of heaven grew,
When of the same white clay God made the dove,
They made you, Lykke, knowing you were fair.

A CARAVAN FROM CHINA COMES

(After Hafiz)

A caravan from China comes;
For miles it sweetens all the air
With fragrant silks and dreaming gums,
Attar and myrrh—
A caravan from China comes,

O merchant, tell me what you bring,
With music sweet of camel bells;
How long have you been travelling
With these sweet smells?
O merchant, tell me what you bring.

A lovely lady is my freight,
A lock escaped of her long hair,—
That is this perfume delicate
That fills the air—
A lovely lady is my freight.

Her face is from another land,
I think she is no mortal maid,—
Her beauty, like some ghostly hand,
Makes me afraid;
Her face is from another land.

The little moon my cargo is.
About her neck the Pleiades
Clasp hands and sing; hafiz, 'tis this
Perfumes the breeze—
The little moon my cargo is.

THE WOMAN OF DREAMS

I am she who comes back and comes back with the sound of the rain,
I am she who whispers and whispers hidden among the leaves;
I am the sea and the wind, and the sigh of the summer grain,
And the lonely reed am I that rocks and whimpers and grieves.

I am the woman who came in the dawn and the dew of your days,
For when first awakened your eyes 'twas upon my face they fell;
From your cradle you rose and walked the world in the hope of my face,
Seeking the woman of dreams, in heaven, in earth, and in hell.

Yes! I am the woman of dreams, the woman no man shall wed—

Would you mate with the rising moon, or the glimmer of stars upon streams?
Or marry the mist on the mere, or the hopes in the heart of the dead?
Then home to your hearth shall you bring me—me, the woman of dreams.

Have you seen a light on the hills you never shall touch with your hand?
Have you heard a voice in your sleep you never again shall hear?
Have you dreamed of a sea so blue, and O of so green a land,
Believed in a tale more true than the stories of eye and ear?

Have you dreamed of a gold and a silver more silver and more gold
Than men mine in the mountains, or deep dived for some dream
Pearl beyond reach of diver, at the spent end to hold
A drowning clutch of radiance, a sinking circling gleam?

I was the gold, I the silver, the light on the hills, the pearl,
The sound of the summer leaves was I, the sound was I of the rain,
The hope in your heart was I, your dream boy's dream of a girl,
Yea, the woman of dreams was I—that all men must love in vain.

Ah! never shall you be mine, beloved, nor ever can I be yours!
You are the kiss of the sun on the sea, I am the flying foam,
Ah! shall we live in a rainbow, love, so long as a rainbow endures.
For I am the woman of dreams, and the rainbow is my home!

III

O climb with me, this April night,
The silver ladder of the moon—
All dew and danger and delight;
Above the poplars soon,

Into the lilac-scented sky,
Shall mount her maiden horn,
Frail as a spirit to the eye—
O climb with me till morn.

Let whoso will sing towns and towers,
'Tis not so that my heart is made,
My world is a wide world of flowers,
Leaf upon leaf and blade on blade.

Of buds and butterflies and birds
I ponder, lying in the grass,
For company, the quiet herds.
And the slow clouds that pass and pass.

Safe in the leafy arms of trees,
I watch, through many a summer noon.
The silken shadows of the breeze.

Till the stars come and bring the moon.

To silent talk of growing things
I hearken with a loving ear,
And all that buds or builds or sings,
Is to my heart beloved and near.

O meadows of the earth so green!
O meadows of the sky so blue!
How happy have these sad eyes been
Just looking my great love at you!

SONG TO THE MOON

Sweet mother moon! for am I not your child?
Kind mother moon! what is your child to do?
For surely there is in me something wild—
And they all tell me that it comes from you.

Here am I lonely as a babe new-born,—
Nothing to bring the world in hard exchange;
A ray too delicate to live till morn,
A phantom in the daylight, lost and strange.

O put a dream into my lunar head—
That I may sell its silver as I sing,
And earn a meal, moon-mother, and a bed,
And buy my bruised lute another string,

THE CUCKOO

O cuckoo troubling yonder hill
With call—and call—and call,
I pray you sing a little low,
If you must sing at all.

You ghost-like bird that breaks the peace
Of April with your cry,
Not spring you mean, for when you come
The spring is near to die.

To me you seem a midnight bird,
A voice of death and doom
That in the palace of the spring
Cries from some haunted room.

The vultures tearing at my heart

Bring no such keen a pang,
Bird with the blossom in your voice,
As though the hawthorn sang.

THE NIGHTJAR

To-night, beneath an operatic moon
I listened to the flattered nightingale,
Ornate, melodious, impeccable—
Round notes of fluted silver soft as dew—
The soul of Tennyson become a bird.

'Twas thus, I thought, that Leighton painted Greece,
Thus fell the moulded notes of Mendelssohn,
Canova thus made marble make-believe—
The very marble colder for his art,

Is this the voice that made the fame of Keats?
Moon of the voices of the voiceless night,
Moon-echo of the sun that is the lark.
Men tell of Itys and thine ancient woe,
Only old grief could wield so new an art—
An art so cold, a studious art of tears,
That charms the taste, but never stirs the soul.

So have I seen a perfect face go by,
Hard wax of measured features without flaw,—
Snow-queens of) beauty, cold as death within.
Faces of smitten metal, chiselled stone.

This patterned song holds nothing for my heart,
I need a more bewildered wistful song,
Agony-made, and warm with hidden tears,
The heart-made music of a heart that breaks.

O nightingale, it is not thine that song—
Water-fall song, a ruined-castle song,
Song of the mouldering minster, glassy lake,
And mossy mountain song.

Great nightingale, there is a toad of sound,
Whose raucous passion until yesterday
Found not a nest in any willing ear;
Browning among the birds, the nightjar he.
Spinning a homespun thread of coarsest song.
Ah! but the mighty rude sincerity,—
Brawny, and bracken-born, and hoarsely sweet,
Song of the hairy heather-honeyed throat.

He recks not of the moon, nor heeds the stars,
He churrs but to his mate and flutters low.
Flits, flaps, from pine to pine, and never tires—
O patient passion! passionate patience! so
Would I too will to wait, and so would sing.

Coarse beak of blunted music, uncouth bird
That grinds monotonous music m the night,
Trusting that truth shall make amends for art;
Thy voice is as the face the future loves,
Face poor in feature, rich in flaming soul.
Rude bird, a shire of pinewoods in thy voice.
Fern-throated, thistle-tongued, and moorland bred.

Thine is the voice of souls, the voice that cries.
Lonely, across the world, for but one voice
That hears and cries again, or never hears;
Voice of the uncouth beauty, of the tongue
Harsh in cold ears, but dulcet to the ear
That loves the voice, and loves no other voice—
All heedless of the accomplished nightingale.

Nightjar, for thee I build a cage of gold.
And here within the palace of the moon.
Where the dark pine makes black the silver ground,
Bird of the heart, my nightjar, sing to me—
While in the valley, sings the bird of brain.

AN EASTER SONG

Arise, my heart, and sing thy Easter song!
To the great anthem of returning bird,
And sweetening bud, and green ascending blade.
Add thou thy word.
Long was the winter and the waiting long;
Heart, there were hours, indeed, thou wert afraid,—
So long the Spring delayed.

Shut in the Winter's alabaster tomb.
So white and still the sleeping Summer lay
That dead she seemed;
And none might know how in her magic side
Slept the young Spring, and moved, and smiled, and dreamed.
Behold, she wakes again, and, open-eyed.

Gazes, in wonder, 'round the leafy room,
At the young flowers. Upon this Easter Day
Awaken, too, my heart, open thine eyes,
And from thy seeming death thou, too, arise.

Arise, my heart; yea, go thou forth and sing!
Join thou thy voice to all this music sweet
Of crowding leaf and busy, building wing,
And falling showers;

The murmur soft of little lives new-born,
The armies of the grass, the million feet
Of marching flowers.

How sweetly blows the Resurrection horn
Across the meadows, over the far hills!
In the soul's garden a new sweetness stirs,
And the heart fills,
As in and out the mind flow the soft airs.
Arise, my heart, and sing, this Easter morn;
In the year's resurrection do thy part,—
Arise, my heart!

FOR SUNDIALS

Shadow and sun—so too our lives are made—
Here learn how great the sun, how small the Shade!

Soon shall the shining circle cease to run;
Soon shall to-morrow turn to yesterday;
That knife of shadow cutting in the sun
Cuts patiently thy light of life away.

NEW-BORN

Frail new-born wings,
Small voice that sings,
New little beating heart,
Dread not thy birth,
Nor fear the earth—
The Infinite thou art:
The sun doth shine,
The earth doth spin.
For welcome—enter in
This green and daisied sphere.
Rejoice—and have no fear.

WAYFARING

Apples along the highway strewn,
And morning opening all her doors,
The cawing rook, the distant train,
The valley with its misty floors;

The hillside hung with woods and dreams.
Soft gleams of gossamer and dew,
From cock-crow to the rising moon
The rainbowed road for me and you.

Along the highway all the day
The waggons filled with apples go,
And golden pumpkins, and ripe corn,
And all the ruddy overflow

From Autumn's apron as she goes
About her orchards and her fields,
And gathers into stack and barn
The treasure that the summer yields.

A singing heart, a laughing road,
With salutations all the way,—
The gossip dog, the hidden bird,
The pig that grunts a gruff good-day;

The apple-ladder in the trees,
A friendly voice amid the boughs,
The farmer driving home his team
The ducks, the geese, the uddered cows;

The silver babble of the creek,
The willow-whisper—the day's end.
With murmur of the village street,
A called good-night, an unseen friend.

TWILIGHT

Strange, at this still enchanted hour,
How things in daylight hard and rough,
Iron and stone and cruel power,
Turn to such airy star-lit stuff.

Yon mountain, vast as Behemoth,
Seems but a veil of silver breath,
And soundless as a flitting moth,
And gentle as the face of death,

Stands this stern world of rock and tree,
Lost in some hushed sidereal dream,—

The only living thing a bird,
The only moving thing a stream.

And, strange to think, yon silent star,
So soft and safe amid the spheres,—
Could we but see and hear so far—
Is made of thunder too and tears.

SONG

Take it, love!
'Twill soon be over,
With the thickening of the clover,
With the calling of the plover,
Take it, take it, lover.

Take it, boy!
The blossom's falling.
And the farewell cuckoo's calling,
While the sun and showers are one,
Take your love out in the sun,

Take it, girl!
And fear no after,
Take your fill of all this laughter,
Laugh or not, the tears will fall,
Take the laughter first of all.

A DITHYRAMBUS OF BUTTERMILK

Let whoso will sing Bacchus' vine,
We know a drink that's more divine;

'Tis white and innocent as doves,
Fragrant and bosom-white as love's

White bosom on a summer day,
And fragrant as the hawthorn spray.

Let Dionysus and his crew,
Garlanded, drain their fevered brew,

And in the orgiastic bowl
Drug and besot the sacred soul;

This simple country cup we drain
Knows not the ghosts of sin and pain,

No fates or furies follow him
Who sups from its cream-mantled rim.

Yea! all his thoughts are country-sweet.
And safe the walking of his^feet,

However hard and long the way,—
With country sleep to end the day.

To drain this cup no man shall rue,—
The innocent madness of the dew

Who shall repent, or frenzy fine
Of morning star, or the divine

Inebriation of the hours
When May roofs in the world with flowers!

About this cup the swallows skim,
And the low milking-star hangs dim

Across the meadows, and the moon
Is near in heaven—the young moon;

And murmurs sweet of field and hill
Loiter awhile, and all is still.

As in some chapel dear to Pan,
The fair milk glimmers in the can.

And, in the silence cool and white,
The cream mounts through the listening night;

And, all around the sleeping house,
You hear the breathing of the cows,

And drowsy rattle of the chain.
Till lo! the blue-eyed moon again.

SPRING

This is the spring,
The time to fling
Sad hearts sky-high!
To sail old hopes
Like kites in the sky,
And take old dreams
From hidden places,

And find old loves
In the new faces.

This is the spring
The time to sing,
The time to wing—
Old flowers come out
With the old blue eyes,
Yet filled anew
With the old surprise,
And not a thing
In the old world dies.

This is the spring,
The time to bring
Love to the folk
That make the flowers.
The lovely faces
In hidden places.
Fast asleep
Through the April showers.

Blue were their eyes.
Blue are the flowers,
Green as the light ascending blade,
Was the hope in the hearts
That laughed and said;
'Are you afraid? '
Forget them not,
This shining day,
The apple-blossom
Is in the sky,—
But, do you forget
That you will die.
That even you
Will some day he
As low as any flower of May.

If only when you come to die.
From your still heart
A song shall rise,
Or from the eyelids
Of your eyes
The moon shall steal out
In the sky,
An unforgetful fragrant flower,
Or from your grave
A butterfly
Flit for an hour.

SONG

Time is very long
Without a song,
Weary is the day,
With love away.

O is there nothing singing,
Is there nothing winging,
Nothing, nothing, flinging
Its warm wild heart away!

If only I could borrow
A rainbow from to-morrow,
To pay the lovely debt
I owe to yesterday,—
Ah! then my head would rest
On young to-morrow's breast.

A SONG OF BREAD AND HONEY

Of all the meals you can buy for money,
Give me a meal of bread and honey!

A table of grass in the open air,
A green bank for an easy chair,

The table-cloth inwrought with flowers
And a grasshopper clock to tick the hours

Between the courses birds to sing
To many a hidden shining string,

And neither man nor maid be seen,
But a great company of green

Upon a hundred thousand stalks
Talk to us its great green talks.

And, when the merry meal is done,
To loiter westward with the sun,

Dipping fingers ere we go
In the stream that runs below.

Of all the meals you can buy for money
Give me a meal of bread and honey!

OCTOBER MOONLIGHT

The moon is up at half-past five,
She frightens me among the pines;
The moon, and only half-past five!
With half the ruddy day alive—
So soon, so high, so cold, she shines,
This daylight moon among the pines.

The moon is walking in the wood,
Her face is very white and strange;
The moon is coming through the wood.
Her face half-hidden in her hood.
Cold silver face whose hourly change
Blanches her cheek more white, more strange.

The moon beneath a pine-tree stands,
Her weary face is full of dreams;
The moon by yonder pine-tree stands,
She builds a palace with her hands,
Pillars of silver, shafts and beams,—
She builds a palace for her dreams.

The moon is sleeping in the trees.
So early is she tired of heaven,
The moon is dreaming in the trees,
Her shepherd boy she sees! she sees!
Asleep, and it is only seven!
O moon, that is so tired of heaven.

NOVEMBER

This year, I said, when first along the lane,
With tiny nipples of the tender green
The winter-blackened hedge grew bright again,
This year I watch and listen. I have seen
So many springs steal profitless away,
This year I garner every sound and scent.
And you, young year, make not such haste to bring
Hawthorn and rose, nor jumble, indiscreet.
Treasure on treasure of the precious spring,
But bring all gently forth upon the air,
Unhasting to the fair.

Yet still the spring escaped me, and once more
I stand in the late autumn's sighing door,
While the dishevelled lone distracted trees

Lose in bewildered sweeps their yellow leaves;
And the birds sing not, nor is butterfly
Pursued of swallow, nor swallow in the eaves,
Long since flown south to warmer climes than these;
And here is but November left and I:
To wonder if the hawthorn 'bloomed in May,
And if the wild-rose with so fine a flush
Mantled the cheek of June, and if the way
The stream went singing foamed with meadow-sweet,
And if the throstle sang in yonder bush,
And if the lark dizzied with song the sky.
I watched and listened, yet so sweet, so fleet,
The mad young year went by.

AT EVENING I CAME TO THE WOOD

At evening I came to the wood, and threw myself on the breast
Of the great green Mother, weeping, and the arms of a thousand trees
Waved and rustled in welcome, and murmured
"Rest— Rest— Rest!
"The leaves, thy brothers, shall heal thee, and thy sisters, the flowers, bring peace."

At length I stayed from my weeping, and lifted my face from the grass;
The moon was walking the wood, with feet of mysterious pearl,
And the great trees held their breath, trance-like, watching her pass.
And a bird called out of the shadows, with voice as sweet as a girl.

And then, in the holy silence, to the great green Mother I prayed:
"Take me again to thy bosom, thy son who so close to thee
Aforetime, filial, clung; then into the city strayed—
The painted face of the town, the wine and the harlotry,

"Bathe me in lustral dawns, and the morning star, and the dew;
Make pure my heart as a bird, and innocent as a flower,
Make sweet my thoughts as the meadow mint—O make me all anew—
And in the strength of beech and oak gird up my will with power.

"I have wandered far, O my Mother, but here I return at the last,
Never again to stray in pilgrimage wanton and wild;
A broken heart and a contrite here at thy feet I cast,
O take me back to thy bosom!"—and the Mother murmured, "Child."

IV

SLEEP FOR LONDON

Only this prayer for London, merciful Lord:
Of all thy bounty just a little sleep,
A little sleep for London, merciful Lord.

There is much sleep in heaven, merciful Lord,
Spare us a little, of thine Infinite Love,
A little sleep for London, merciful Lord.

See her so worn and weary, with her head,
Like some tired sempstress, fallen on her arm,
Trembling awake at any least alarm,—
She dreams, poor soul, dreams sweetly she is dead.
With no more morns for ever, merciful Lord.

We ask no great thing, Lord,
None of thy splendid answers unto prayer;
Only a little sleep—she is so worn,—
Some intermission of implacable morn,
Nothing more great or splendid beg for her,
Only a little sleep, merciful Lord.

Only a little holiday of sleep,
Soft sleep, sweet sleep; a little soothing psalm
Of slumber from thy sanctuaries of calm,
A little sleep—it matters not how deep;
A little falling feather from thy wing,
Merciful Lord,—is it so great a thing?

Lo! in the east, with cruel face of steel,
Day the taskmaster cries the abhorred hour.
And wakens London with the lash of dawn.
Merciful Lord, dawn comes not so in heaven,
Nor steals it so o'er many a rich man's lawn—
Kind-hearted nymph, soft-footed as a flower.
That with her dews night-weary eyes would heal—
Is there indeed a land where dawn is sweet?

Here morn flies bloody down each London street,
The fury Dawn that hates to see men rest—
Of all thy good, great Lord, deep sleep is best;
A little sleep for London, merciful Lord!

THE THAMES

River of Death that divides implacable foes for a little,
Keeps, so I fable, the hand of the East from the throat of the West,
Thames that puts on her jewels this frivolous lute-stringed twilight—
Mark yon crescent of pearls from the Minster clock to the Tower,
Mark her bracelets of light, her beautiful golden bridges,

Mark the moons in her hair, and her palaces down to the water:
And mark over there on the dark other side of her flowing,
Stretched at black length, a formless and cowering monster.
Here and there a small eye lit in the night of his strength—
Wafted over to him little frightened waifs of the laughter.
'Tis the Leviathan Labour watching there in the darkness,
Watching and waiting the hour to spring with a roar from his dockyards,
Tear down those honeycombed lights and burn up the butterfly people.
Break them, and burn them, and quench them down there in the River of Death.

LONDON BEAUTIFUL

London, I heard one say, no more is fair,
London whose loveliness is everywhere,
London so beautiful at morning light
One half forgets how fair she is at night,
London as beautiful at set of sun
As though her beauty had but just begun;
London, that mighty sob, that splendid tear,
That jewel hanging in the great world's ear.
Strange queen of all this grim romantic stone,
Paris, say some, shall push you from your throne.
And all the tumbled beauty of your dreams
Submit to map and measure, straight cold schemes
Which for the loveliness that comes by chance
Shall substitute the conscious streets of France,
A beauty made for beauty that has grown,
An alien beauty, London, for your own.

O wistful eyes so full of mist and tears,
Long be it ere your haunted vision clears,
Long ere the blood of your great heart shall flow
Through inexpressive avenue and row;
Straight-stepping, prim, the once adventurous stream.
Its spirit gone, it loiters not to dream,
All straight and pretty, trees on either side,

For London's beauty London beautified.

Ah! of your beauty change no single grace,
My London with your sad mysterious face.

A FAREWELL TO LONDON

London, that long our loves may last,
Let's part awhile, beloved town,
I need the peoples of the breeze,

The conversation of the down.

I hear the sea that calls me home,
And the wild, wild bird that whistles me,
And I must go and meet to-day
An unforgotten faithful tree.

Back to my palaces of air,
Where all day long green fountains play,
Back to the singing uplands pure
And the clear call at break of day.

The short sweet nights, the long sweet days,
The innocent madness of the dew,
The sun's great brimming cup to drink,—
Then back, my London, back to you.

BROOKLYN BRIDGE AT DAWN

Out of the cleansing night of stars and tides,
Building itself anew in the slow dawn,
The long sea-city rises: night is gone,
Day is not yet; still merciful, she hides
Her summoning brow, and still the night-car glides
Empty of faces; the night-watchmen yawn
One to the other, and shiver and pass on,
Nor yet a soul over the great bridge rides.

Frail as a gossamer, a thing of air,
A bow of shadow o'er the river flung,
Its sleepy masts and lonely lapping flood;
Who, seeing thus the bridge a-slumber there.
Would dream such softness, like a picture hung,!
Is wrought of human thunder, iron and blood?

V

"TO LOVE!"

To love!
That is my prayer—
Gifted to love,
Just the old simple everlasting way:
Of all life's gifts
That is the gift I crave.

I ask not kindness,

I ask not any gift or any grace,
Or any charity;
The love I mean
Is not for you to give or take away.

That you are cruel
Shall be no less provocative
Than that you're kind,
And whether you remember or forget
Shall to the love I crave
Be equal lure.

I ask not nearness,—
You are ever near;
I ask not sympathy
In common aims,
I ask not comprehension,
I ask not anything.

Only I pray to love,
And bring my heart
Gladly for you to break—
If break it can—
Gladly to feel your fair contemptuous feet
Grind it beneath you
In the passionate dust.
Yea, break my heart,
For that were ecstasy!

Think not 'tis you I crave,
You to possess, command, nay! nor to serve;
My love would not be kind,
Nor live in offices of tenderness;
You to the thing I crave
Are but the accident from which it springs.

It is not admiration.
It is not gratitude,
It is only love—
A madness,
A glory burning in the lonely brain,
A fearful fire filling the lonely heart.

To love, to love, to love!
Is this the way?

"HOPELESS OF HOPE, PAST DESIRE EVEN OF THEE"

Hopeless of hope, past desire even of thee,

There is one place I long for,
A desolate place
That I sing all my songs for,
A desolate place for a desolate face,
Where the loneliest land meets the loneliest sea.

Green waves and green grasses—and nought else is nigh.
But a shadow that beckons;
A desolate face.
And a shadaw that beckons
The desolate face to the desolate place
Where the loneliest sea meets the loneliest sky.

Wide sea and wide heaven, and all else afar,
But a spirit is singing,
A desolate soul
That is joyfully winging—
A desolate soul—to that desolate goal
Where the loneliest wave meets the loneliest star.

"O LOVE, I LOOK ACROSS THE SEA"

O love, I look across the sea,
The sails go by,
From vastness into vastness fade,
Lost in the sky.

O the great world I so wide and cold,
And you so far!
If only you could come as near
As yonder star.

Aloft, alone, I vex it not
With me or mine;
So far—yet am I near enough
To see it shine.

For lack and love of you, love,
I pine the long days through;
I waste the powers
Of the rich hours,
For lack and love of you.

For lack and love of you, love,
All life is grown untrue;
O I squander
And wander,
For lack and love of you.

For lack and love of you, love,
I grow myself untrue;
I am drowning,
Drowning, drowning.
For lack and love of you.

"TRUE HEART"

True heart,
True heart,
I have no joy but thee—
Sugared delights may be,
And coloured toys;
But my enduring joys
Must come from thee,
Always and always, love,
Must come from thee.

"LONG AFTER YOU ARE DEAD"

Long after you are dead
I will kiss the shoes of your feet,
And the long bright hair of your head
Will go on being sweet;
In each little thing you wore
We shall go on meeting, love;
In a ring we shall meet,
In a fan we shall meet,
Or a long-forgotten glove.
Long after you are dead,
O the bright hair of your head,
And the shoes of your little feet!

"OF ALL THE DAYS WE SAID THAT DAY WAS GOOD"

Of all the days we said that day was good,
When, 'neath the blue publicity of heaven,
Amid the flickering marguerites we stood,
And gave—or thought we gave—what once is given
And only once is taken quite away.
But, child, since then how rich the months that passed
With child-glad hours and many a perfect day,
Nor maybe yet the happiest or the last.

Yet, love, I wonder if the day we went

Up that high tower, and stood up in the sky,
Yet unto earth returned again, was meant
To symbolise our love; nay, even I,
In a dim-lighted, unbelieving hour,
Have wondered if we really climbed the tower!

"I DID NOT KNOW THAT I LOVED YOU, LOVE, LIKE THIS"

I did not know I loved you, love, like this:
I thought our love was chance and passing need;
Your eyes were very brown, and, O your kiss
Was sweet indeed—
Yet dreamed I not of loving you like this.

You stole so unannounced into my life,
No fatal premonitions or alarms
Told me that you were my star-chosen wife;
There were your arms—
And unannounced I stole into your life.

Had some one asked me of you, I had said:
"It is too late to meet her—long ago
She is a dream, or maybe she is dead;
I do not know
More to tell any of her," I had said.

And now, beloved, too well you know the rest—
One woman must be heaven, and earth, and hell;
So soft, yet so responsible, a breast!
I said "Too well"—
Love, is my head too heavy for your breast?

"I LIE AWAKE TO WATCH YOUR SLEEPING FACE"

I lie awake to watch your sleeping face,
And listen to your tender-taken breath;
Only at times I shudder—
For your sleep seems so like death.

"GRACE O' GOD"

Grace o' God,
Flower face,
Silver feet,
In what place.

Heaven or earth.
Did we meet?
At what time
Of the day?
In what way?
Was it near.
Was it far,
In some star,
Or just here,
Quite, quite near?
Tell me, dear—
Grace o' God,
Tell me, dear.
Grace o' God,
I know well
When we met;
It was first,
Grace o' God,
When I knew
I loved you—
Then we met—
That was just,
Grace o' God,
Flower face.
Silver feet;
When I first
Looked—O looked I
On your face—
Silver feet,
Golden heart,
Grace o' God.

"I HEARD A LIAR SAY MY LOVE DOTH CEASE"

I heard a liar say my love doth cease,
Heart of my heart, because sometimes I rest
My burning head upon some other breast,
Seeking in all this hell a little peace,
A little comfort in this long disease
Of loss I suffer, loss by them unguessed
Who find in the new-born East for long-lost West
Sufficient heaven. I am not of these.

But, sometimes, when the life I may not kill
Grinds pitiless iron on the screaming nerve,
I cry for woman as ether, woman as wine,
Lest Death's black poppies in my hair I twine:
Thus faithful, faithless, work I on until
Finished the bidding of the saint I serve.

"GIVE ME THY TEARS"

Give me thy tears: I ask not for thy kiss,
Or for thy smile—but only for thy tears;
Take where thou wilt thine hopes—give me thy fears;
Lavish on shallower loves thy time of bliss:

But when it ends,—and naught so certain is
As bliss doth end—though it be years on years
Though 'twere the hour before the last hour nears,
Come to me then—I ask no boon but this.

"O LET THEM WATCH"

O let them watch at corners and peer and smell,
Those starveling sneak-thieves of the human heart,
Selling their little lies in some foul mart,—
I have a miracle no man can sell,
A wonder that no thieving tongue can tell;
The secret is: how beautiful thou art.
The four winds cannot blow us two apart,
And we care not whether 'tis heaven or hell—

Knowing the time is now so very soon
When we shall sit at each end of the moon,
Our two hands safe together across the sky;
Laughing at that pathetic world below,
That said it knew and yet could never know,—
How could it know, down there in its sad sty!

Ah! sweet, the cruel world—
How cruel it is!
How much we pay it
For a simple kiss—
The silly world, as if we wouldn't pay
More than the world can give or take away!

But, love, there is one toll that we must pay,
When the dark ferry-boat on the dark stream
Rows us both softly back from dream to dream.

"WAS IT FOR THIS WE MET—TO PART LIKE THIS"

Was it for this we met—to part like this;

Was it for this we loved—to lose this way;
Can this be April reddening into May,
And will the woods grow green and never miss
Beneath their boughs the murmur of our bliss,
The happy children of a summer day;
Was it for this we loved—to lose this way;
Was it for this we met—to part like this!

O little haunted river, will you run
Still through the trees and leap the rocks in foam,
Yet hear no more our voices blent with yours;
If thus the painted scene of love endures,
Earth's floor of flowers and heaven's azure dome,
O can the play be ended—quite, quite done!

"I LOVE HER NO MORE. I WOULD HAVE DIED"

I love her love no more. I would have died
For her least need, but of her cruel whims
I am no slave. Man is too much a god
To worship even a woman utterly:
This let one woman learn and one man teach.
A man is woman and a man besides,
A woman only woman.

"ALL THE LOVING EVER DONE"

All the loving ever done
Is not so sweet as the kiss o' the sun,
Nor a woman ever born
As good to look on as the morn.
Up, my soul, and let's away
Over the hills at break of day.
Following, whatever befalls,
Yonder fairy horn that calls,
Angel-blown in yonder star;
Better far, O better far,
Better far than any girl.
Is the morning's face of pearl,
And the wind about our ears
The true music of the spheres,
And the running of the river
Good to listen to for ever.

"HOW MANY FRIENDS I LOVED ARE GONE"

How many friends I loved are gone
Death delicately takes the best:
O Death, be careful of the rest!
I cannot spare another one,—
So many friends I loved are gone!

THE TRAVELLER

'Twas moonrise on the Tenth of May,
I met a traveller walking fast;
I touched his arm and bade him stay—
"Old friend, we meet at last."

All tall and dark and strange he seemed
Under the rising moon,
He turned and said—"I never dreamed
That we should meet so soon.

"You are too young to be my friend,
All hope and boyish breath;
Are you quite sure you know my name? "
"Your name," I said, "is— Death."

"I SAW A ROSE IN MY GARDEN BLOWING"

I saw a rose in my garden blowing—
I said, "O rose, where art thou going?"
Answered the rose: "Where the stream is flowing,
And all the winds of the world are blowing,—
Where thou thyself art also going."

"Rose," said I, "will it come to pass,
When your petals fall upon the grass,
That you some dewy morn again
Will press your cheek at my window-pane?"
The rose's answer was, "Alas I"

THE WAY OF A DREAM

I had a dream, and it went this way—
It went the way of a bird in the air,

It went the way of the butterfly,
It went the way of the moon in the sky,

It went the way of all things fair:
It went to dwell with a sleeping face
That rests in a hidden marble place,

Where no foot falls, no word is said,
Only sometimes a bird will call,
Or a little wintry leaf will fall.
Or a snowdrop lift its head.

LIFE

Life is that doomed, mysterious, sad-eyed flower
That through the cosmic granite, like a rose.
Pushes its dewy stem, and for an hour
In the stern sunshine of existence blows.

MARJORIE AND THE SPRING

I said: It is the spring, Marjorie!
But she never heard;
I said: There is the thrush, Marjorie!
But she never cared;
I said: Come, see the crocuses,
How fine they flame!
But she never came.
I said: Where art thou, Marjorie?
Dost thou not hear,
O He-a-bed, O sleepy-head,
That spring is here?
Come in your gown of gold and green
To meet the king!
Three springs in vain to Marjorie
This song I sing;
But she never hears, and she never cares,
And she ne'er will come,
For Marjorie is dead, yea! blind s Marjorie,
Yea! deaf is she and dumb.

"I HEARD DEATH ON A SUMMER DAY"

I heard Death on a summer day
Go singing up the street:

I turned to an old friend and said,
"Was ever voice so sweet!
O see the poppies in his hair—
And his alabaster feet!"

HIC JACET

I whose strength was like a tower
Am now a little blue-eyed flower,
A blade of grass, an April shower.

I whose arm was strong as ten
Am weaker than the little wren,
Or a drop of churchyard rain.

I whose face was once all light,
All dreams and boyhood and delight,
Cover my face up in the night.

MY FRIEND

I have a friend who is dead—
A wonderful friend is he:
He knows I am lonely and living,
So he spends his time with me.

He forsakes the shining gardens,
And all the rainbowed dead,
To sit and talk and comfort me—
For living—my friend who is dead,

"TIME CANNOT TAKE AWAY"

Time cannot take away
What Time did give;
Sad as our hearts may be,
We once did live;

And, howso robbed, who knows
But those strange friends,
Death and Eternity,
May make amends.

TO MRS. LANGTRY, ON HER DEPARTURE FROM AMERICA

I do not bring you flowers,
Or singing birds,
To say farewell,
Nor even words;
Nor to the altar of your eyes
Do I bring sighs;
Such antiquated tribute
To the youth
Of the eternal Spring
I do not bring.
And, surely—stars above!—
I bring you not
That miracle called love:
All I can bring—
The one gift worthy you—
Is to bring back again
The wonder and the joy and the delight
Of mortal eyes that saw a little while
The loveliness immortal.
I that am poor in all that is not you
What can I do
Save bring you back yourself
As offering!
Had I but pain
Then would I bring that too—
Alas! there is no pain
For me and you.
So all I bring,
As tribute to your feet,
Is that most precious thing
The joy you gave,
Indifferently sweet
As some bright star,
That shines alike on all,
And shines for none alone;
Shines but for shining's sake
In the high heaven afar.
Fair star, too soon to sink
Behind the sea,
My little hoard of star-dust
Here I bring,
As offering:
You unto you—from me.

EX LIBRIS

. . . multum ille et terris jactatus et alto,
Vi superum, saevae memorem Iunonis ob tram:
Multa quoque et hello passus, dum conderet urbem,
Inferrefque deos Latio; . . .

Having no home, what should I do with these,
Tossed as I am about the sounding seas,
Sport of exiling winds of change and chance—
Feet in America, and heart in France.
Homeless, 'tis meet I find my books a home:
Coffined in crates and cases long they lay,
Distant from me three thousand miles of foam
Dungeoned in cellars cold and nailed away,
As in a sepulchre, till Judgment Day,
Lost to their gentle uses in the tomb,
Cobwebbed companions of the spidered gloom,
At last they rise again to live once more,—
Dread resurrection of the auction room.

Books I have loved so well, my love so true
Tells me 'tis time that I should part from you,
No longer, selfish, hoard and use you not.
Nor leave you in the unlettered dark to rot,
But into alien keeping you resign—
Hands that love books, fear not, no less than mine.

Thus shall you live upon warm shelves again,
And 'neath an evening lamp your pages glow,
Others shall press 'twixt leaf and leaf soft flowers.

As I was wont to press them long ago;
And blessings be upon the eyes that rain
A tear upon my flowers—I mean on "ours"—
If haply here and there kind eyes shall find
Some sad old flower that I have left behind.

AN EPITHALAMIUM ON THE MARRIAGE OF WILLIAM FAVERSHAM AND JULIE OPP

No one to-day is happy as you are,
No one so happy in any place or land,—
Not in sea-hidden islands ringed with spray,
Nor yet in any impregnable bright star,
Nor any girl or boy.

Nearest approached to your beatitude
Are we who watch your wonderful glad eyes

Here at the awful gates of Paradise;
Our hungry hearts eager with gratitude—
Only to look on the rare face of joy.
O Will! Oh Julie! do you understand?
This is the day!

Do you remember how the long days wore?
So long, so many, so empty, and so slow;
It seemed indeed that they could never go:
And O! the lonely sound of all that sea!
The days will not be empty any more,
And you shall search the calendar in vain,
Nor find one long day in the longest year;
Yes! pray some god to make them long again—
O you will never have one minute to spare
From the grave business of felicity!

Husband and wife! O happy, happy pair!
A anion so perfect that it seems
A fabled bliss, a marriage made in dreams,
A rainbow strangely painted on the air.
Husband and wife—those old unhappy words
Glow with mysterious blessedness once more,
Like an old world made young again with flowers.
And the green leaf and the returning birds,
And the warm murmur soft of gleaming showers—
Young April packed with sweetness to the core.

Young king and queen,—pass to your palace now;
Pass in and from your happy windows gaze
Along your stately avenue of days.
Survey the shining gardens of your peace
And all the future filling with increase
Of garnered joy, and prosperous with praise—
The long sweet ripening of your marriage vow.

ON SOME RECENT EDITIONS OF OSCAR WILDE

These are the poems of that tragic one,
Who, loving beauty much, loved life too well;
Therefore, to-night he makes his bed in hell.
Gone are the grace and glory—all is gone;
The tower is fallen that so proudly shone
In the sun's eye, and now the hucksters sell
The sculptured stone, foul groping where it fell—
O ruin fair for ghouls to batten on!

Maggots in the decay of the divine,
Ghouls of the printing-press, ere yet he died

You spat your little venom on his name,
You who now pick and pillage in his fame,
Robbing the pockets of the crucified:
But the great silent talker makes no sign.

ON THE ASSASSINATION OF PRESIDENT McKINLEY

This is no way to freedom: to smite down
Some unoffending head that wears a crown—
Only to set it on a sterner brow.
Not I of those who dream the world's release
Will come by the soft processes of peace,
Or the pacific compromise of power;
And when at last dawns the stern bloody hour,
When the slave stands with rifle in his hand,
And sweeps the master from the stolen land,
I too would hold a rifle in my hand.
But when that day dawns we shall fight like men,
Glad men that laugh because at last they see
So close the blazing eyes of those they hate—
In honesty of hate his life or ours,
His death or ours in honesty of hate.
We shall not sting an unsuspecting heel,
Or fire into an unprotected breast:
This is no way to freedom—it were best
Another hundred years to wait and wait,
Then flash into the sun the fearless steel.

A PRAYER

Out of the deeps I cry to thee, O God!
I fain would bring my soul safe up the sky—
This shining jewel rainbowed like a tear,
This star in the body that belongs to heaven.
With all the straining strength of my poor might,
I stagger with it up the dreadful way—
O but I fear unless some succour comes,
Some kindness of some angel, or some help
From watching planet sad to see me climb.
That in some gulf the precious thing must fall.
For I am weak and weary, and all my will
Went in the miles behind me, and no more
Remains in me to face the frowning height.

Ah! is my soul, that is so much to me,
Nothing to thee, O God?
See in my hands that I stretch up to thee

The lovely thing thou gavest: let it not
Die ere I die—but rather pluck its light
Out of my brain, while still it brightly burns,
Not with my body gutters to decay.
Out of the deeps I cry to thee, O God!
I fain would bring my soul safe back to thee.

"IF THOU HADST NOT BEEN BORN"

If thou hadst not been born, if this fair day
Had not illuminated all the year,
Shining like diamond in the calendar,
If Time were empty of this date divine,
And grim November robbed of its one flower, what of me!

If thou hadst not been born!
How strange the thought, how lonely to the heart
Whose future is all written in thine eyes.
Whose past was but a prophecy of thee!

If thou hadst not been born!—Ah! but thou wert!
And God was good to me, and of His grace,
In this same garden of time thou makest sweet
Gave me to wander, seeking for my flower.

Attlar of all the roses of the world.
Enchanted flower that in the mystery
Of one perfection hides all perfect things.
Given to him who loves thee in thy face.

Richard Le Gallienne – A Concise Bibliography

My Ladies' Sonnets and Other Vain and Amatorious Verses (1887)
Volumes in Folio (1889) poems
George Meredith: Some Characteristics (1890)
The Book-Bills of Narcissus (1891)
English Poems (1892)
The Religion of a Literary Man (1893)
Robert Louis Stevenson: An Elegy and Other Poems (1895)
Quest of the Golden Girl (1896) novel
Prose Fancies (1896)
Retrospective Reviews (1896)
Rubaiyat of Omar Khayyam (1897)
If I Were God (1897)
The Romance of Zion Chapel (1898)
In Praise of Bishop Valentine (1898)
Young Lives (1899)

Sleeping Beauty and Other Prose Fancies (1900)
The Worshipper of The Image (1900)
The Love Letters of the King, or The Life Romantic (1901)
An Old Country House (1902)
Odes from the Divan of Hafiz (1903) translation
Old Love Stories Retold (1904)
Painted Shadows (1904)
Romances of Old France (1905)
Little Dinners with the Sphinx and other Prose Fancies (1907)
Omar Repentant (1908)
Wagner's Tristan and Isolde (1909) Translator
Attitudes and Avowals (1910) essays
October Vagabonds (1910)
New Poems (1910)
The Maker of Rainbows and Other Fairy-Tales and Fables (1912)
The Lonely Dancer and Other Poems (1913)
The Highway to Happiness (1913)
Vanishing Roads and Other Essays (1915)
The Silk-Hat Soldier and Other Poems in War Time (1915)
The Chain Invisible (1916)
Pieces of Eight (1918)
The Junk-Man and Other Poems (1920)
A Jongleur Strayed (1922) poems
Woodstock: An Essay (1923)
The Romantic '90s (1925) memoirs
The Romance of Perfume (1928)
There Was a Ship (1930)
From a Paris Garret (1936) memoirs
The Diary of Samuel Pepys (editor)

www.ingramcontent.com/pod-product-compliance
Lightning Source LLC
Chambersburg PA
CBHW060055050426
42448CB00011B/2468